Ancient Origins of Modern Technology

From Chariots to Rockets

Table of Contents

Chapter 1. Introduction

Unearth the fascinating lineage of modern technology in our Special Report: "Ancient Origins of Modern Technology: From Chariots to Rockets." This delightful journey traces the first sparks of human innovation, revealing how our ancestors ingeniously solved problems, the echoes of which reverberate in the devices and vehicles we use today. From the thrill of the first wheel revolution to the glory of space exploration, discover how we're standing on the shoulders of ancient geniuses. If curiosity hasn't yet tickled your fancy, let us assure you that this report is teeming with enthralling revelations and compelling narratives, guaranteed to leave you in awe of humanity's historical inventiveness. You'll be eager to get your hands on this enlightening voyage through time, a read that serves as a spectacular reminder of man's indomitable spirit of discovery. Reserve your copy now and let your mind journey across millennia of invention and ingenuity!

Chapter 2. Inception of Innovation: Unearthing Earliest Technology

Our story begins at the dawn of time, when man first crawled out of the primal soup of existence and looked towards the sky with intelligent eyes for the first time. With these eyes, he began to study his world, the rocks, the trees, the animals. He quickly learned to use these elements to his advantage, using them to create tools that would aid his survival.

2.1. The Stone Age: Primitive Tools and Techniques

During the Stone Age, humans began to create tools. Tools are a defining hallmark of human evolution, separating us not only from our closest primate relatives but also setting us on a path of unstoppable innovation and discovery. The earliest found tool, appropriately named the 'Oldowan,' after the Olduvai Gorge in Tanzania where it was discovered, dates back to approximately 2.6 million years ago. Primarily composed of rocks and stones, these primitive tools were used for cutting, chopping and scraping, making survival a tad bit easier for our ancestors. But, what's even more striking is the cognitive leap these early humans took - turning ordinary rocks into purposeful tools.

2.2. Harnessing Fire

Following stone tools, humans took another leap toward modern technology by learning to control fire. The exact timeline is still disputed by scholars, but available evidence suggests this could have occurred around 1 million to 1.5 million years ago. Fire provided warmth, a means to cook food, and a method to ward off predators. Enhanced diet and safety have been pivotal in our evolutionary trajectory. Fire use marks a significant turning point in human evolution, a stride towards civilization.

2.3. The Wheel: The Round Revolution

While exact dating is subject to debate, it's widely accepted that the wheel was invented around 3500 B.C in Mesopotamia, today's Iraq. Resources suggest that the wheel likely originated as the potter's wheel before being applied to transport applications. This simple yet ingenious invention sparked the wheels of trade and transport, bringing far-off civilizations together. The wheel has stood the test of time and is still an essential component of numerous modern-day technologies.

2.4. Metallurgy: The Birth of Alloys

While humans enjoyed a productive relationship with metals from as early as the Stone Age, extracting and manipulating metals into tools and weapons did not become commonplace until around 5000 BC. This period, known as the Bronze Age, saw humans transition from stone to bronze in manufacturing tools, impacting agriculture, war, and art. The widespread use of refining techniques and the invention of new materials marked a significant stride in technological prowess.

2.5. Writing: The Dawn of Information Age

Writing systems, believed to have first surfaced around 3200 BC in

Mesopotamia, revolutionized human communication and record-keeping. Early forms of writing utilized pictographic symbols before transitioning to cuneiform – wedge-shaped symbols pressed into clay tablets. This marked another significant leap in the civilizational story, as the advent of writing systems allowed for the transfer of knowledge across generations.

2.6. Ancient Engineering: The Awe-Inspiring Accomplishments

As we moved from the Bronze Age to the Iron Age, mankind's technological capabilities surged forward dramatically. Ancient civilizations such as the Greeks, Egyptians, and Romans produced engineering marvels – buildings, aqueducts, roads, and other infrastructures - that showcased their cognitive prowess and aesthetic sensibilities. These served societal needs and stood as a testament to human brilliance, some of them still standing tall, centuries later.

This journey into humankind's earliest ventures into technology paints an encouraging picture. Our innate ability to innovate and adapt has been the driving force behind human progress, pushing us from being mere foragers to becoming space explorers. This propensity for curiosity and invention, born in the crucible of prehistoric survival, pulses through the veins of modern technology and continues to shape our world in incredible ways. The story of technology is the story of humanity – an unending odyssey of learning, curiosity, adaptability, and resilience. It's a testament to the human spirit, indomitable and ever-defining in its quest for betterment.

Chapter 3. The Wheel and the Chariot: Revolution that Redefined Motion

Man's pursuit of facilitating motion has forever been marked by an understanding of nature and its resources, consistently stretched to limits by human ingenuity. Adorning the crown of such inventions is the wheel - an innovation so profound, it revolutionized human existence by redefining our understanding of motion.

3.1. Experiments with Rolling: The Genesis of Motion

Around 3500 B.C., in the land now known as modern Iraq, the visionaries of ancient Mesopotamia, struck with the simplicity and efficacy of natural round objects rolling down a slope, envisioned the first wheel. Fashioned out of wood, stone, and eventually metal, these were rudimentary but significantly improved human capability to transport goods and services far beyond their reach.

The initial wheels were not meant for transportation; pottery wheels were among the earliest applications. Clusters of clay representing the axle and the wheel itself were connected and spun using manual force. It was only around 3200 B.C. when the wheel was attached to a chariot, paving the way for a monumental shift in motion and transportation.

3.2. The Adoption and Advancement: Wheel, Axle, and Chariot

The early wheel-and-axle concept faced several issues - friction being the most prominent. Yet, it was evident that the advantages of its suitability for transportation far outweighed its drawbacks. Realizing the wheel's potential, the chariot, a two-wheeled, horse-drawn vehicle, was developed.

The chariot was a celebrated invention of its time. Besides its practical use, it was also a symbolic cultural icon. From religious rituals to royal processions, from battles to sports events, chariots carved their importance in the society of the age.

3.3. Vitruvius' Wheel: The Transformation Begins

Around the first century B.C., the renowned Roman engineer and architect Vitruvius proposed a water wheel design, thereby marking the wheel's transition to power utilization. This pioneering albeit forgotten innovation was the cornerstone for mechanized gain in human society.

Despite the wheel being sidelined for other technological developments during the Dark Ages, its potential was reidentified with the onset of the Industrial Revolution. Society woke to the realization that not all power need be human or animal generated. The waterwheel and windmill became cornerstones of the era, providing power for a variety of tasks.

3.4. From Wood to Rubber: Material Evolution

From the ancient Mesopotamian stone wheels to the wooden wheels of the medieval era, wheels had seen little change in their fundamental design. However, the Industrial Revolution brought new demands, and rubber, with its resilience, durability, and grip, was introduced to the wheel design. The development of pneumatics led to the inflatable rubber tire, impacting transportation in a radical way.

Later, the creation of synthetic materials allowed for even greater efficiency and durability. Most contemporary tires consist of chemical compounds such as styrene and butadiene, improving longevity, fuel efficiency, and safety.

3.5. Chariots to Mode T: Wheels in Modern Transportation

It would be remiss to talk of wheels without touching on their impact in modern transportation. The automotive industry, by pairing the internal combustion engine with the wheel, made personal transportation widely accessible.

The Ford Model T, arguably the ancestor of the modern car, brought wheels closer to everyone. Its assembly line production allowed mass distribution and led to improved wheel design, including the demountable rim for easy tire replacement.

3.6. Defining Aeronautics: Wheels that Roll Above the Clouds

The contributions of the wheel extend far beyond roadways. Aviation would be unachievable without landing gear – critical wheel-based systems. Wheels allow planes to taxi, takeoff, and land, making commercial aviation possible.

3.7. One Giant Leap: Wheels on Lunar and Martian Soils

The lunar rovers of the Apollo missions reconfigured wheels for operation under reduced gravity, extreme temperatures, and rugged terrains. Despite the moon's harsh conditions, wheels were still the most viable mobility option. Decades later, when humanity set its sights on Mars, wheels played an essential role. The Mars rovers have their lineage from the first wooden wheel of antiquity.

In conclusion, while the underlying principles of the wheel have remained largely unchanged, its significance in our society has not. Today, we see their sophistication in everything from the cars we drive, the planes we fly in, to the Mars rovers exploring uncharted terrains, bearing testament to the genius of our forebears. The wheel, in many ways, is a chronicle of human progress - a testament to our imaginative spirit and the drive to make the impossible possible. Far from becoming obsolete, the wheel will continue to evolve and serve as a vital cog in the machinery of human advancement.

Chapter 4. Harnessing Liquid Fire: The Ingenuity of Ancient Metallurgy

To delve into the annals of history is to plunge into a saga of remarkable human endeavors. The story of ancient metallurgy is a perfect epitome of humankind's inventive spirit, exemplified by the harnessing of materials to forge tools, weapons, and objects of majesty and utility.

4.1. The Dawn of Discovery

Our journey begins in the Neolithic era, the age of polished stone tools. The people of this era were cultivators and herders, living in established settlements rather than leading nomadic lives. Even at this stage, human innovation heralded a rudimentary understanding of metallurgy. Copper beads unearthed from archaeological sites in Northern Iraq dating back to around 9000 BC serve as the earliest evidence of metalworking.

Copper, found naturally in a virtually pure state, was shaped and hammered into tools, weapons, and ornamental artifacts. This marked the advent of the Copper Age, or Chalcolithic period, that spanned several millennia.

4.2. From Copper to Bronze

The evolution from Copper to the Bronze Age approximately around 3300 BC is significant as it represents one of the earliest instances of alloy development. Bronze—an alloy of copper and tin or arsenic—possesses superior hardness and durability compared to pure copper. This innovative breakthrough transformed society and culture, with effects rippling outwards across all strata. Bronze tools and weapons were far superior to their stone contemporaries, catalyzing a shift in balance of power and instigating territorial cultural advancements.

The existence of immense temperature gradients in the smelting process meant that the raw materials underwent a dramatic transformation from their solid state into a fiery liquid, before they were cast into their final form—an appropriately poignant symbol of the transformative impact of metallurgy on our ancestors' lives.

4.3. Cultural Mosaic of Metallurgy

The smelting techniques and skills developed rapidly as cultures absorbed knowledge from each other. Trade routes during the Bronze Age connected disparate tribes and nations, facilitating the exchange of metals, ideas, and innovative practices. Through this integrative process, metalworking artistry and expertise flourished across the Mediterranean and toward the British Isles, interweaving various cultural strands into a richly diverse metallurgical tapestry.

4.4. Iron Age: Strength and Supremacy

As time marched on, humanity harnessed the superior qualities of iron around 1200 BC: a landmark event marking the onset of the Iron Age. Stronger, more abundant, and versatile than copper or tin, iron became as crucial to societal development as the discovery of fire.

The widespread adoption of iron had a profound influence on the development of civilization, leading to advancements in agriculture, weaponry, and construction. Cities and empires rose and fell on the strength of their iron-wielding prowess.

4.5. Technological Evolution and Legacy

As human understanding of metallurgy evolved, so did technological capabilities. Alloys such as steel, an iron and carbon combination, became essential components in construction, mechanical engineering, and, eventually, the production of modern-day automobiles and skyscrapers.

The ability to control fire and use it for the purpose of transforming and manipulating metals was a remarkable feat of ancient civilizations. The echoes of this innovation still reverberate throughout our modern world, transforming how we live, work, and interact.

The legacy of ancient metallurgy reaches far beyond tools and weapons, shaping societies and cultures, and ushering in the dawn of civilization. The ingenuity demonstrated by our ancestors in harnessing 'liquid fire' didn't just change the trajectory of their own lives but redefined the destiny of humankind.

The fascinating secrets embedded in ancient metallurgy extend a clear line to the technological advances we enjoy today. To understand the origin of our devices, machinery and building materials is to appreciate the richness of human endeavor and the incredible journey we embarked upon when we first sought to control the elemental force of fire. This chapter is but a singular filament in the broader tapestry of inventiveness, one among countless others that we'll continue to explore.

Chapter 5. Ancient Architectural Marvels: Mastering Materials and Mathematics

Imagine the ancient world with its grandeur and marvel— pyramids piercing the skies in Egypt, the formidable Great Wall snaking its way across Asian landscapes, Greek temples showcasing elegance with mathematical precision, and the daunting Roman aqueducts marking an era of extraordinary engineering ingenuity. These structures stand resilient even today, evidence of the past's architectural prowess. Let us explore how humanity's early pioneers laid the foundation for modern architecture, defying the limits of materials and mathematics in their creations.

5.1. Mastery of Materials: Stone, Clay, and Wood

Stone, clay, and wood were the earliest materials employed by mankind to fabricate shelters and monuments. Crafting rudimentary tools, our ancestors managed to manipulate these materials into shapes and forms, which would evolve into masterpieces over the millennia.

Dwelling initially in makeshift shelters made of wood and hide, humankind quickly discovered the durability of stone as a construction material. The iconic megalithic structures—like the Stonehenge in England and dolmens scattered across Europe—signal the dawn of a new age. Stones were not merely stacked but arranged using rudimentary principles of balance and weight distribution—a testament of early understanding of physics.

The ancient Egyptians took this a notch higher with their refined stone-cutting techniques, carving out intricate shapes and designs on stones for their monumental structures, the pyramids. These colossal edifices were not just tombs, but cosmic diagrams reflecting the Egyptians' astronomy knowledge. The alignment of these structures to the cardinal directions and celestial bodies shows their understanding of geography and astrology.

Meanwhile, humans were also mastering the art of turning clay into bricks—parable to a caterpillar's metamorphosis into a butterfly. The ancient city of Mohenjo-daro thrived on this brick technology, with its well-planned cityscape, featuring houses, granaries, and an elaborate drainage system built entirely of uniformly-sized, kiln-fired bricks.

5.2. Mathematical Genius in Architecture

Now that we've scratched the surface of material mastery, it's time to voyage into the world of numbers, angles, and proportions to unlock the mystery behind these architectural wonders.

The precise alignment and symmetry showcased in the ancient world's architectures required knowledge beyond basic arithmetic. Geometry, believed to have originated in the river valleys of Egypt and Mesopotamia, became a vital tool for architects.

Sundials and obelisks of Egypt reveal the ancients' sophisticated understanding of angles. The meticulous measurements encoded in the iconic Pyramid of Giza suggests a working knowledge of the Pythagorean theorem, long before Pythagoras was born.

Further west, in the classical era, the Greeks displayed their command over mathematical proportions and harmony through their temples. The Parthenon, particularly, illustrates the Golden

Ratio's application in its façade, with ratios of lengths meticulously calculated to achieve aesthetic perfection.

5.3. Magnificent Building Techniques

The ideas behind the construction techniques in antiquity were as groundbreaking as the structures themselves.

The Egyptians used simple machines like ramps and levers to shift and hoist heavy blocks to construct their pyramids. It reflects a nuanced understanding of force and motion—an elementary form of what we now understand as mechanical engineering.

In the ancient city of Petra, the Nabataeans pioneered a 'carving from top to bottom' technique. This method ensured the preservation of the natural structure and avoided cave-ins while creating majestic rock-cut architectures.

The Romans exhibited extraordinary engineering skills in erecting their colossal structures. The Pont du Gard aqueduct was assembled using precisely cut stones and gravity—the water flowed downhill due to a gentle gradient maintained across miles! The Colosseum, made of concrete and stone and spanning 189 meters in length, stood as a testament to their remarkable feat in mastering complex construction techniques.

5.4. A Beacon of Innovation: Architectural Achievements

The pioneering use of arches, domes, and vaults to create structures with large-spanning interiors was an epoch-making innovation. Romans were masters of these methods, which made construction of their baths, basilicas, and amphitheaters possible.

Domes—a magnificent blend of materials and mathematics—define the ancient architectural skyline. The Greeks integrated self-supporting domes topped with an 'oculus' or eye into their designs, exemplified by the Pantheon's magnificent, freestanding dome.

Vaults, primarily barrel and groin, enabled the creation of intertwined corridors and thermal baths, far beyond the capabilities of flat roofs. The Romanesque and Gothic architectures later heavily integrated them.

Axum, in Ethiopia astonished the world with their monolithic structures. These structures – tall, towering, and carved out of a single piece of stone – mark the epitome of aesthetic expression and architectural dexterity.

As we traverse the millennia from the rudimentary shelters to the grand structures of the ancient world, we begin to grasp the monumental leaps in technology, materials, and mathematical concepts. These jumps shaped our understanding of the universe and our place in it. They facilitated the transition from fundamental practical needs to a deep appreciation of aesthetics, culture, and spirituality that so defines us as humans.

The ancient world's awe-inspiring architectural marvels continue to inspire architects and dreamers alike to this day. Each structure—an echo from our past—holds within its stones and bricks, a story of human curiosity, courage, and ingenuity. They are a testament to humankind's indomitable spirit and unyielding desire to push the boundaries of the possible. This thread of innovation, seamlessly woven through the fabric of time, connects us to our ancestors and will continue to pierce the veil of the future.

Chapter 6. Eclipsing Epochs: From Sundials to Grandfather Clocks

The tale of time telling, like so many others, winds its way back to the earliest cradles of human civilization. Diverse cultures, independently, developed unique methods to track, measure and harness time to their advantage, all of which have fed into the myriad ways we understand and keep time today.

6.1. Sundials: The First Steps

In the shadows of early civilization, sundials emerged as the first devices to measure the passage of time. The principle behind a sundial is deceptively simple, predicated upon the predictable movement of the sun across the sky. The Greeks are often credited with pioneering these ancient timepieces, yet sundials saw use long before their time. As far back as 1500 BC, the Egyptians had already erected obelisks that, while grandiose in their own regard, could double as massive sundials.

To an observer's eye, a sundial would consist of two main components: the style or gnomon, a rod or thin plate which cast a shadow, and the dial, the surface marked with lines indicating the hours of the day. As the sun moved, the shadow of the gnomon would fall onto these hour lines, providing an estimation of the time.

The simplicity and efficiency of the sundial have echoed through millennia, and their basic design can still be seen in gardens and public spaces all over the world today.

6.2. The Invention of Water Clocks

As humanity progressed, so did our need for more intricate timekeeping mechanisms. Sundials, for all their elegance and ease of use, had one crucial flaw: they were dependent on sunlight. Therefore, they weren't effective at night or during cloudy days. Thus, the water clock, or clepsydra, was born somewhere around 1500 BC.

The ancient Greeks, Egyptians, and Chinese independently developed these early devices, which measured time's passage through the regulated flow of water. Water from a higher vessel would drip at a steady rate into a lower one, or water would spill from a hole in a vessel, and the time was told by observing the water level within.

With the advent of water clocks, time tracking became more reliable and maybe, for the first time, became independent of natural phenomena. Our ancestors became creators of time in their own limited yet profound manner.

6.3. The Wonderful World of Weight-Driven Mechanisms

The steady evolution of timekeeping devices led to the adoption of weight-driven mechanisms. From the mechanical escapements of ancient Greece to the incipient escapement mechanisms of medieval Europe, these contrivances represented significant leaps forward in the journey from sundials to modern clocks.

It's believed that the earliest escapements came from Greece, as part of the famous Antikythera mechanism. However, it was in the monastic communities of medieval Europe where weight-driven clocks had their true flowering moment. These were important for the monks to comply with their canonical hours and were, therefore, placed in clock towers often annexed to churches or monasteries.

6.4. The Grandeur of Grandfather Clocks

The journey of timekeeping from sundials to water clocks and weight-driven mechanisms culminated grandly in the development of pendulum clocks or as they are lovingly referred today, the Grandfather clocks.

In the 1650s, Christiaan Huygens, a Dutch scientist and horologist, transformed timekeeping by incorporating Galileo's study of pendulums into his design of a weight-driven clock. Huygens' precision with the pendulum clock was unprecedented for its time - deviating less than 15 seconds per day.

Aesthetically too, grandfather clocks have held their own. With their tall, freestanding and often ornately carved wooden cases, they remain a symbol of old-world charm and elegance, a representation of humanity's indomitable quest to capture time, and a testament to the exciting journey from sundials to the present.

From the simple sundial to the grandeur of grandfather clocks, our history is a testament to an unwavering human resolve to master time. This journey had not only marked human understanding of time but also carved the path for modern horology. Every tick of the hand today traces back through a time where hours and minutes were decided by the shadow's dance on a sunlit day. Everytime you glance at your wristwatch or smartphone today, remember, it's a legacy handed down to us across millennia, by ingenious minds who dared to challenge and change their world. Fifty millennia later, their spirit still reverberates within every second, minute, and hour we track, in the ceaseless march of time.

Chapter 7. Scripting Success: Writing Systems and the Birth of Record Keeping

The ability to have language, a sophisticated form of communication, has long differentiated humanity from other life forms on Earth. This unique trait came to its own in the creation of writing, a revolutionary system that allowed human thoughts, ideas, and expressions to be recorded and preserved across time and space.

7.1. Evolving Communication: Symbols to Script

From the earliest times, our ancestors sought ways to communicate that extended beyond immediate verbal interaction. Proto-humans first used markings on bones and cave walls to communicate valuable information on survival: strategies for hunting, mapmaking, and messaging to others - generations after generations.

The earliest known form of writing is seen in the shape of ancient cave paintings that date back to around 40,000 years ago. These were simple depictions of life at the time, portraying the local wildlife, hunting methods, or social and religious rituals. Non-verbal communication took a more specific shape as humans adopted pictograms and ideograms- simple pictures and symbols that represented ideas, objects, or events. Cultures like the Sumerians and Egyptians in 3500-3000 BC took this further into early script, utilizing a system of symbols and characters, allowing for more complex and specific communication.

7.2. From Sumerian Ingenuity to Egyptian Innovation

Sumerians in Mesopotamia are credited with the development of the world's first comprehensive writing system - 'cuneiform'. Around 3200 BC, this script was initially pictographic, just like its predecessors. However, cuneiform evolved to represent sounds using wedge-shaped marks made on clay tablets, marking the first time humans recorded spoken language.

The Egyptians' answer to the Sumerians' cuneiform came a few centuries later around 2690BC, with hieroglyphs, inspired by the need to cater to a different language with different phonetic needs. Hieroglyphs were unique in that they could be used as both logograms (a character that represents a word or phrase) and phonograms (a character that represents a sound), through more stylized and abstract characters and symbols.

7.3. The Rise of the Alphabet

Despite the effectiveness of logographic systems, these early writing forms were complex to master. A simplified system was desired, leading to the development of the earliest forms of the alphabet in the Near East. Ugaritic script and the Phoenician alphabet are among the earliest examples of such simplified systems and a precursor to many modern scripts.

The Phoenicains, a seafaring people, spread this simplified writing system through their extensive trading networks, making it a base for many others. The Greek alphabet, often considered the first true alphabet as it marked vowels and consonants distinctly, borrowed heavily from Phoenician writing around 800 BC. The later Romans adapted the Greek alphabet to their own language, giving rise to the Latin alphabet that is now the most widely used writing system in the world.

7.4. Scripts of the East: The Chinese Miracle

Around the same time as the Sumerians, Chinese civilization developed its unique writing system. The earliest known Chinese character inscriptions, from around 1250 BC, were 'oracle bone' writings, etched on turtle shells and animal bones. These characters were a complex mix of ideographic, pictographic, and later phonetic symbols.

With over 50,000 characters (though an educated person might only need to know around 5,000), Chinese script stands apart due to its foundation on ideas rather than phonetics. Even today, while multiple languages and dialects are spoken across China, the written language remains virtually standard.

7.5. A New Dawn: Scripts and Modern Society

Writing systems evolved rapidly through the ages, with the development of paper and the printing press accelerating literacy and the distribution of written work. Modern society was fundamentally shaped by the ability to codify laws, preserve history, propagate religions, and share scientific breakthroughs. The birth of writing propelled us from transient oral traditions to durable, transmissible, and accumulative knowledge, forever transforming humanity's collective intellectual journey.

Today, writing and record-keeping are integrated into every facet of our lives, from education to social interactions, businesses, sciences, and the arts. Indeed, scarcely can we imagine a world without written text - a testament to the monumental human achievement in the form of script and the enduring legacy of our ancient inventors.

Chapter 8. Sailing Through Century: Maritime Technology and Ancient Trade

The ancient maritime world was distinguished by its vibrancy, complexity, and sophistication. Seafaring, the lifeblood of ancient civilizations, served as a conduit for trade, cultural exchange, and warfare. As ancient people became seasoned mariners, they devised and perfected technology to give them the edge in navigating the occasionally rough and perilous waters. Harnessing the wind for propulsion, crafting nautical equipment for direction and communication, they were able to traverse perilous oceans with confidence.

8.1. The Birth of the Sea Vessel

The story of maritime technology commences with the invention of the sea vessel. The oldest known boat, a simple dugout canoe unearthed in the Netherlands, is estimated to be around 10,000 years old. Made from a hollowed-out log, it illustrates our ancient ancestors' instinct to exploit bodies of water. Initially, boats were propelled by human power—paddles and eventually oars. This made travel slow and laborious but also meant that sailors had reliable control over their trajectory.

As civilizations grew more sophisticated, so did their maritime technology. The Egyptians, for example, advanced from fishing boats paddled or rowed in the Nile to larger, sturdier riverboats and seagoing ships. They utilized papyrus plants to construct light, sturdy vessels, often featuring a square sail.

8.2. The Winds of Change: Sailing

The invention of the sail was a pivotal moment in maritime history. It transformed sea travel from an exhausting, man-powered ordeal into a more efficient and far-reaching endeavor. The earliest known depictions of sails are found in Egyptian art dating back to around 3500 BCE. These sails were square-shaped, hung from a yard (horizontal spar), and used to catch wind from behind — a downwind sailing.

The Phoenicians, unrivalled mariners of the ancient Mediterranean world, made significant advancements in sailing technology. Their sails were hewn from a patchwork of animal hides or linen, and unlike their Egyptian counterparts, these were designed to defeat the wind rather than merely follow it. This "beating" or "tacking" to the wind enabled Phoenician vessels to travel more consistently and predictably.

8.3. Perfecting the Vessel: Design and Material

The design and material of the ship made a profound difference in navigation capabilities, ranging from riverine crafts, coastal vessels, and blue-water trading ships to colossal war galleys. The vessels of ancient Greece were usually wooden, of either pine, fir, or oak, and built in the "shell-first" technique. They boasted a sleek design with far-reaching triremes, vessels propelled by three banks of oars to allow for effective warfare.

Roman naval architecture was heavily influenced by the Carthaginians whom they conquered in the Punic Wars. Romans developed the "corvus," a mobile boarding bridge that allowed their soldiers to board enemy ships, effectively turning sea battles into land battles where they dominated.

Meanwhile, the Vikings' longships, with their shallow draft and aerodynamic design, were marvels of technology and craftsmanship. Masterfully designed for open sea navigation and war incursions, these vehicles could also navigate rivers and streams, allowing the Vikings to penetrate far into the countryside.

8.4. Navigation and Communication

Maritime technology wasn't just about the vessels but also about the tools that facilitated the journey. Early navigators used landmarks and the stars for direction. As their voyages extended into open sea beyond the sight of land, they developed new navigation techniques employing celestial bodies.

The Phoenicians likely used the North Star (Polaris) to navigate. The Greeks developed the "gnomon," a vertical stick that cast a shadow, allowing them to determine their latitude based on the shadow's length at noon.

Moreover, maritime communication evolved from basic methods like smoke signals or flags to sophisticated systems like the Greek hydraulic telegraph in the 4th century BCE, a hydraulic system that signaled coded messages over long distances.

8.5. The Impact of Maritime Technology

The effects of maritime technology on ancient civilizations cannot be overstated. It enabled trade networks that spanned continents, disseminated cultural practices, and allowed for far-reaching warfare and colonization. In ancient Rome, the harbors of Ostia and Portus stood at the end of the world's largest network of sea routes, bringing goods from as far away as India and China. These hubs linked the Roman Empire with the wider world, exhibiting the crucial role maritime technology played in the very fabric of these societies.

Maritime technology's legacy persists today, from the basic designs of our boats and ships to our navigation techniques. It was a field where the ancient world exhibited great innovation, shaping civilization in ways that still resonate. Therefore, an exploration of maritime technology in the ancient world is truly a voyage through the currents of human history and invention that have perpetually shaped our story.

Chapter 9. Sky's Not the Limit: The Telescope and Space Exploration Beginnings

In humble observatories across seven centuries and the depths of space, spanning across human history and beyond our earthly confines, our understanding of the cosmos has shifted dramatically, due in no small part to the advances in one pivotal instrument: the telescope. We invite you to embark on this thrilling odyssey, tracing the progress of astronomical viewing devices and the unraveling of cosmic mysteries, kicking off with the telescope's invention and marking milestone moments of space exploration.

9.1. A Glimpse into the Starry Canvas: The Invention of the Telescope

It all began in the humid air of a Dutch spectacle workshop in the early 1600s, where one Hans Lippershey filed for a patent for a device that could 'make faraway objects appear closer.' Little did he know that this rudimentary instrument, a tube with a pair of concave and convex lenses, would transform humanity's relationship with the cosmos.

Lippershey's device reached the hands of one Galileo Galilei who, with typical ingenuity, improved upon the design. With his enhanced 'spyglass,' Galileo turned his sights towards the sky and made discoveries that challenged contemporary thought and scientific principles. Discovering the craters on the moon, the many moons of Jupiter, and the phases of Venus shattered the geocentric worldview and cemented our heliocentric reality.

9.2. A Quantum Leap: Reflective Telescopes and the Herschel Era

As we stepped into the 18th century, telescopes evolved from refractive to reflective. Sir Isaac Newton deserves credit for this innovation, utilizing a curved mirror instead of a lens to gather and focus light. Without Newton's ingenuity, we would have been left grappling with the stubborn problems refracting lenses presented, which included chromatic aberration — an issue that compromised the clarity of celestial observations.

The reflective telescope marked the dawn of an era, taking us from observing visible planetary bodies to peeking into deep space. William Herschel, along with his sister Caroline Herschel, used these immense and highly sophisticated Newtonian reflectors to discover the planet Uranus and numerous comets, expanding humanity's knowledge of our solar system.

9.3. Unveiling the Unseen: The Haynes Telescope and Spectroscopy

In the late 19th century, Alvan G. Clark, an American astronomer, polished a lens that would be lauded as the 'Great Lick Reflector.' This enormous device, mounted on Mount Hamilton in California, was a considerable milestone in telescope technology. Yet, the true innovation was not just in the size but also in the new way astronomers started observing stars.

Edward C. Pickering and his team at the Harvard College Observatory initiated spectroscopy, exploring the properties of celestial bodies beyond mere reflected light. Spectroscopy allows for determining an object's chemical composition, temperature, density, mass, and relative motion.

Quite literally, this analytical tool broke open the light, revealing the rainbow within and taking us steps closer to understanding cosmic objects in a way that is unimaginable with the naked eye.

9.4. A Jumpy Signal: The First Radio Telescopes

In the early 20th century, we entered the era of radio astronomy. First proposed by Karl Guthe Jansky in the 1930s, observing celestial bodies with radio waves opened up a new gateway into the universe's vast expanse. This innovation extended our sense of sight far beyond its biological limitations, facilitating the viewing of non-visible wavelength radiation.

From here, the persistent thrum of celestial bodies became part of our observations. We eaves-dropped on the universe, and the universe had much to say. Radio telescopy uncovered quasars, pulsars, cosmic microwave background radiation, and clarified our understanding of the Milky Way's structure.

9.5. The Great Beyond: Launch of Hubble Space Telescope

From ground-based to space-based, we arrived at another juncture in our journey. The launch of the Hubble Space Telescope in 1990 created a revolution unlike any before. Hovering above the Earth's atmosphere, this space telescope was no longer hampered by atmospheric distortions, orbital radio noise, or light pollution, common issues that plagued earth-based observation.

The spectacular images Hubble produced were a testament to the vast strides telescope technology had made. From capturing the mesmerizing whirl of the galaxies to the dazzling spectacle of nebulae, Hubble unraveled cosmic mysteries and provided valuable data for thousands of research papers.

9.6. Beyond Hubble: New Frontiers

We find ourselves today on the thresholds of new discoveries. Tomorrow's telescopes, like the James Webb Space Telescope, will not only inherit the legacy of their predecessors but also explore the cosmos like never before. With scheduled missions to Mars, the outer reaches of our solar system, and even distant 'exo-planets,' one thing is clear - the sky's indeed not the limit.

As we take this cosmic journey, let us remember that each innovation, each discovery, and each unanswered question, is part of our unquenchable thirst for understanding. Our humble beginnings with Lippershey's rudimentary device now extend beyond our planetary boundaries. The telescope, a testament of human curiosity and the need to explore, has revealed to us a cosmos that is inspiring, breathtaking, terrifying, and beautiful.

Remember, every glance upwards into the night sky connects us with generations of stargazers and the pioneers in astronomy. As we look beyond the reaches of our solar planet, we not only observe the cosmos, but we celebrate the audacity of human ingenuity.

Chapter 10. Ancient Echo in Modern Medicine: Foundation of Health Care

In the annals of civilization, every era is marked by its own unique scientific and technological advancements. The medical field must be recognized as a sterling example of this cycle of progress, and while innovative and seemingly on the precipice of modernity, the groundwork was laid millennia ago.

10.1. Understanding Our Ancient Ancestors: Primordial Medical Practices

Ultrasound and CT scans may be the watchwords of modern diagnostics, but the origins of such techniques can be traced back considerably farther, to a time when shamans used observational diagnostic methods, often credited as "spiritual divination." These techniques, along with a rich apothecary of herbs and plant-based medicines, established the rudimentary framework of healthcare systems. We might call them simple, yet they were but the early scaffolding for the complex and intricate structures of today's healthcare.

The ancient Egyptians were instrumental in shaping the foundational methods of medical diagnostics and treatment procedures still in use today. Papyrus documents from as far back as 1600 B.C. show an uncanny resemblance to contemporary instruction manuals, describing the symptoms of various diseases, the methods used to diagnose them, as well as suggested remedial procedures - medication, surgery, and even arguably psychiatric advice. This underscores the clear link between the earliest documented medical practices and modern ethos, highlighting the continuance of invaluable wisdom over the ages.

10.2. Birth of Modern Medicine: Greek Ascendancy

While the Egyptians were sowing early medical seeds, it was the ancient Greeks who can be considered the inventors of 'modern' medicine. Hippocrates, often revered as the father of medicine, emphasized the importance of careful observation and the application of logical reasoning in disease diagnosis. Discarding the prevailing spiritual and metaphysical explanations of the time, Hippocrates urged the study of the human body for answers.

The famous Hippocratic Oath, a vow undertaken by all medical practitioners today, is a testament of the Greek legacy in the medical field. The theories propagated by Hippocrates were later organized into a holistic medical system by Galen, another Greek physician. This Galenic physiology dominated the medical world until the Renaissance, casting a long shadow over healthcare practices worldwide - a clear indication of the enduring impact of ancient Greek realizations on contemporary medical thinking.

10.3. Medicine under the Roman Banner: A Structural Advancement

While Greeks set a benchmark in medical understanding, it was under the Roman banner that medicine flourished by leaps and bounds in terms of organization. They introduced public health initiatives, developed sophisticated surgical tools - some of which bear remarkable similarity to surgical equipment used in modern times - and prioritized sanitation, understanding its link to disease prevention.

Roman sanitary infrastructure, such as aqueducts and sewage systems, was a medical marvel of the time. They also established mobile medical units to cater to the battlefield casualties, echoing the present-day concept of emergency medical services. The advent of hospitals, albeit exclusively to cater to the gladiators, marked the beginning of institutions solely devoted to healthcare and patient care – the predecessors of our modern hospitals.

10.4. Ayurveda and Traditional Chinese Medicine: The Eastern Inventiveness

As much as the West contributed to the evolution of healthcare, the East wasn't far behind. In India, Ayurveda, a comprehensive system of medicine, was propounded during the Vedic age. The principles of Ayurveda, focusing on the balance of body, mind, and spirit, can be seen in the present-day emphasis on holistic health and the recognition of mental health's importance.

Simultaneously, in China, traditional Chinese medicine (TCM) was maturing with core ideas such as Qi, yin and yang, and the Five Phases, which also illustrated the notion of harmony within the individual and between the individual and his or her environment. Despite being millennia old, TCM is still prevalent and has influenced modern medicine's approach, particularly in the therapeutic domain – acupuncture is a shining example of this continuity.

To summarize, the nuanced, technological world of modern medicine isn't springing from vacuum; it owes a considerable debt to the wisdom and inventiveness of our ancestors. From Egyptian manuals to Greek rationale, Roman organization to Eastern holistic approach, each provided an instrumental building block in the vast structure that is today's healthcare system. This is the true testament to mankind's indomitable spirit of discovery, a journey across time that continues to shape the ever-evolving field of medicine and healthcare.

Chapter 11. Bridging the Ages: How Ancestral Innovations Propel Our Future

In the timeline of human civilization, we encounter a panoply of evidence attesting to the ingenious and ceaseless innovations of our ancestors. This vast cascade of development stretches from the dawn of our species to the present, giving birth to the technological marvels that shape our world today.

11.1. The Genesis of Innovation: The Wheel

The nucleus of our technological timeline is arguably the invention of the wheel. Created around 3500 BC in the area we now call the Middle East, it was a transformational development that revolutionized aspects of human existence like transportation, warfare, and commerce. The wheel, in all its simplicity, stood as a testament to mankind's ability to observe, ideate, and innovate. Even today, its echoes manifest in the most exalted of human endeavour: space exploration.

With every jostle and bump experienced during a car ride, we witness a phenomenon brought to fruition over five thousand years ago. Despite various improvements over the centuries, the fundamental design: a circular object on an axle, remains unaltered. Today, it acts as the cornerstone of numerous vehicles, from lunar rovers trundling on the moon, to Martian rovers exploring the red planet.

11.2. The Fire That Kindles Civilization: Metallurgy

While the wheel set things in motion, it was the discovery of metallurgy that built civilizations. Around 8000 BC, humans started experimenting with naturally occurring metals like gold and copper, giving birth to a revolution that allowed them to create increasingly complex tools, weapons, and architectural structures.

The bronze and iron ages that followed testified to the escalating sophistication of our ancestors' skills. The remarkable transformation of raw, earth-embedded resources into gleaming, durable, and practical tools testified to mankind's ascending mastery over nature and materials. Modern machinery owes an incalculable debt to this ancestral legacy, with critical components made of various alloys, a testimony to our ancestors' first forays into the realm of metals.

11.3. Harnessing the Winds: The Mastery of Sailing

The mastery of sailing is another testament to the innovative mindset of our ancestors. The ancient Egyptians were known for their remarkable ship-building expertise. In 3200 BC, their vessels traversed the Nile with an elegance and certainty borne of skilled engineering and an intimate understanding of the river's capricious temperament.

These ancient mariners continued to refine their craft, leading to the creation of the sail. The sail, a brilliant manipulation of nature's forces for human advantage, facilitated long-distance journeys and spurred global exploration. Modern shipping, enjoying the privilege of technologically advanced propulsion systems, still utilizes the sail, particularly in recreational and competitive domains.

11.4. A Leap into the Future: Energy Generation

Our ancestors also demonstrated an affinity for harnessing natural energy sources. Water wheels and windmills of ancient times were forebearers to today's hydroelectric plants and wind farms, converting kinetic energy into mechanical power for various applications such as grinding grain or pumping water.

Jump forward to the industrial revolution, and the predilection for using steam as an energy source still echoes in our modern power generation methods. Nuclear and coal power plants, the backbone of our energy grid, operate on the principle of driving steam turbines to generate electricity. Simultaneously, renewable energy technologies, like solar panels, represent an evolving effort to capture nature's power more sustainably, representing the latest advancements in an age-old human endeavor - harnessing nature for our needs.

11.5. Age of Flight

Though it took us many millennia to conquer the skies, the roots of modern aeronautics are firmly burrowed in ancient times. The inspiration may have possibly been nature itself, birds soaring in the sky, unbounded and free. This dream, harbored in countless human hearts throughout our history, took a practical form as early as 400 BC, with the advent of the kite in China.

Over the course of centuries, myriad attempts were made to realize this dream. Notably, in the 1480s, Leonardo da Vinci conceived an ornithopter, a machine designed to mimic bird flight. It may have never flown, but it exemplified the enduring human aspiration for flight. Centuries later, the Wright brothers' success in 1903, armed with internal combustion engine technology and rigorous experiments, heralded the age of aviation we inhabit today.

11.6. Ancient Computations Echoes in Modern Computing

Even the roots of the digital world we inhabit today are ancient. The first known analogue computer, the Antikythera mechanism, was developed by Greek scientists around 150–100 BC. This intricate system of gears and dials served as a complex astronomical calculator, tracking the phases of the moon, predicting eclipses, and even marking Olympic games.

Several centuries later, during the 19th century, Charles Babbage conceptualized the Analytical Engine, a mechanical device capable of arithmetical calculations, considered as a blueprint for the modern computer. However, the ENIAC, constructed in 1945, marked the dawn of the digital age, an era that our current technology ecosystem, perched on the shoulders of ancient computational genius, continues to evolve.

Our journey across the timeline of human innovation has testified to a potent thread of continuity. From wheels to computers, we trace our lineage back to these first sparks of inspiration and invention. As we peer into the future, standing at the zenith of human technological capability, our journey continues, still powered by the renewable fuel of human creativity and the spirit of unyielding innovation. This voyage through time manifests a simple truth; we are the echo of our past, reflecting the brilliance of our ancestors on the canvas of the present, projecting it into the limitless realm of tomorrow.